Pop Culture Paganism

Secret Idols in Everyday Life

Karajah Yashar

PASSED
OVER
PRESS

TRUTH BEYOND TRADITION

Orlando, FL 2025

www.passedoverpress.com

ISBN: 978-1-962691-55-0

Table of Contents

Introduction

The Paganism You Don't See

Walk into any American home on a Friday night and you'll notice something. The television is on, maybe Netflix is running. A birthday party at the neighbor's house down the street features a cake, candles, and kids shouting, "Make a wish!" Later that night, a group of friends heads downtown for a bachelorette party—alcohol, risqué games, and maybe even fortune-telling cards. Saturday brings a college football tailgate, complete with ritual chants and painted faces. Sunday morning? Millions gather in churches, but the very day itself is named after the worship of the sun.

We don't think twice about any of this. But we should. Because what passes for harmless fun—or even sacred tradition—in modern pop culture often has roots in something very different: paganism. That's not a conspiracy theory. That's history.

The Unseen Story

The word pagan comes from the Latin paganus, meaning "country dweller." For centuries, before and after the rise of Christianity, ordinary people worshiped the forces of nature, carved idols from wood and stone, and prayed to a dizzying cast of gods. Rome had its Jupiter, Mars, Venus. The Norse had Thor, Odin, Freya. The Celts called on their sun and moon deities. These gods demanded rituals—dances, feasts, sacrifices, charms—that promised luck, fertility, and protection.

4

When the Roman Empire fused politics with religion, these rituals didn't vanish. They adapted. They slipped quietly into European life, then colonial life, and eventually into American culture. What we see now as "normal" is often the repackaging of ancient superstition.

Paganism in Plain Sight

Birthday candles? Straight from ancient Greece, where people offered cakes to Artemis, goddess of the moon. Fortune cookies and horoscopes? Old Babylonian star-worship, recycled. Wedding rings, tossing rice, and veils? Fertility rituals meant to summon blessing from gods of the harvest. Valentine's Day? Once a fertility feast for the god Lupercus, complete with animal sacrifice and wild celebrations.

Even the days of the week betray the hidden truth. Wednesday honors Woden, the Norse god of wisdom. Thursday? Thor, god of thunder. Friday? Freya, goddess of love. These names aren't Biblical. They're pagan. Yet we live by them, structure our calendars around them, and rarely stop to ask why.

Why It Matters

Now, let's be clear. Lighting a birthday candle doesn't make someone a devil worshiper. But ignoring history makes us blind to how far culture has drifted from its biblical roots. Jesus warned about "the traditions of men" replacing the commandments of God. The Apostle Paul described spiritual strongholds—patterns of thinking that keep people in bondage. When we look closely, we see that many modern customs are not neutral. They're spiritual leftovers, designed to shift devotion away from the Creator and toward the created.

That's what this book is about. We're going to pull back the curtain on modern pop-culture paganism. We'll examine bachelor parties, carnival parades, tarot cards, holiday traditions, lucky charms, and much more. Each chapter will uncover where these customs came from, why they persist, and how they subtly shape the way we live and worship today.

Because history isn't just in the past. It's all around us—on our calendars, in our homes, and in our celebrations. And it's time to ask: Are we following God, or are we following gods we don't even realize we're serving?

Chapter 1
Pagan Roots in Everyday Life

Part 1: The Calendar of the Gods

It's astonishing when you stop and think about it. The Bible says flat-out, *"Make no mention of the name of other gods, neither let it be heard out of thy mouth"* (Exodus 23:13). Yet, every time we talk about the days of the week, we are literally speaking the names of false gods. Sunday for the sun god. Monday for the moon goddess. Tuesday for Tiw, a Norse war god. Wednesday for Woden (Odin). Thursday for Thor. Friday for Freya (or Venus). Saturday for Saturn. Seven days, and five of them are named for pagan deities.

That means almost every single day, with casual conversation, people are calling on the names of false gods. "See you on Thursday" is really "See you on Thor's Day." "I'll call you Friday" is "I'll call you on Freya's Day." Imagine how crazy this is: the very thing God warned His people *not* to do is built into the rhythm of our speech. And because tradition normalizes it, we don't even realize we're doing it. It's like a subtle chant to idols that slips under the radar.

The enemy knows that repetition is power. If he can make you call on pagan names every day without thinking, he's already blurred the line between truth and tradition. The Bible says, *"In all thy ways acknowledge Him"* (Proverbs 3:6), but the world has arranged it so that in all our ways, we acknowledge idols. It's a daily reminder of just how deeply pagan roots run in modern culture—and how urgently God's people need to wake up, separate the holy from the profane, and call only on the name of Yahweh.

Imagine trying to explain your weekly planner to the prophets of Israel. "Okay, Isaiah, I'll see you on Thor's day, but I can't stay too long because Saturn's day is booked. Oh, and don't forget Freya's day—big party." Isaiah would probably look at you like you'd lost your mind: "Wait—you plan your whole life around pagan gods? You literally set your appointments on the calendars of idols?" It'd be comedy if it weren't true. We laugh at people bowing to statues, but we still bow our speech to the names of their gods every single week.

And the worst part? Most people don't even know. They'll argue with you about sports stats or movie plots, but ask them who Thursday is named after and they draw a blank. Meanwhile, they're walking around saying "Thor's Day" like they've got a Norse Mythology membership card. Imagine telling someone, "Sorry, I can't make Bible study tonight, I'm too busy honoring Odin's day." That's how crazy tradition gets—it sneaks idolatry right under our noses and makes it sound like ordinary scheduling.

The Days of the Week

Sunday – The Day of the Sun

Ancient Rome called it *dies Solis*—the day of the Sun. The sun was worshiped everywhere: in Egypt as Ra, in Babylon as Shamash, and in Rome as Sol Invictus, the "Unconquered Sun." In 321 A.D., Emperor Constantine, a sun-worshiper turned Christian convert, declared Sunday the official day of rest. He didn't choose the biblical Sabbath. He chose the day of the sun.

Did You Know? Constantine's law in 321 A.D. reads: *"On the venerable day of the Sun let the magistrates and people* *residing in cities rest."* That's the origin of Sunday worship in Western culture.

Monday – The Day of the Moon

Monandæg in Old English. *Lunae dies* in Latin. Pagan cultures honored moon goddesses—Artemis in Greece, Diana in Rome, Ishtar in Babylon. The moon controlled tides, fertility, and harvests, and people bowed to it. Today, you just call it Monday.

Tuesday – The Day of Mars

The Romans named it *dies Martis*, after Mars, god of war. The Norse called it Tiw's Day, for their war god Tyr. Same god, different name. Either way, Tuesday is dedicated to bloodshed and battle.

Wednesday – The Day of Mercury

Mercury was the Roman messenger of the gods, linked to speed, travel, and trickery. The Norse knew him as Woden or Odin, chief of their gods. That's why we say "Wednesday"—Woden's Day. Your midweek slump has a pagan chief god stamped on it.

Callout: Every time you say "Wednesday," you're invoking Odin, the one-eyed Norse god.

Thursday – The Day of Jupiter

To the Romans, it was *dies Jovis*—Jupiter's Day. To the Norse, it was Thor's Day, honoring the hammer-wielding god of thunder. Today Thor's a Marvel superhero. Back then, he was worshiped in blood-soaked rituals.

Friday – The Day of Venus

Romans called it *dies Veneris*, Venus's Day. Venus was their goddess of love and sex. The Norse honored Freya, goddess of fertility. Every Friday, people unknowingly tip their hat to a goddess once celebrated with orgies and fertility rites.

Saturday – The Day of Saturn

Saturn was the Roman god of agriculture and time. His feast, Saturnalia, was a week-long carnival of drunkenness, gift-giving, and immorality. The echoes of it remain every December when we celebrate Christmas. Saturday still carries his name.

The Months of the Year

The pagan roots don't stop at the days. Flip to your calendar's months, and you'll find gods and emperors there too.

- **January**: Named after Janus, the two-faced Roman god of beginnings and endings. He looked both forward and backward, overseeing transitions. Every New Year's resolution? Dedicated to him.

Did You Know? Ancient Romans sacrificed to Janus every January 1st, asking him to bless the coming year. That's where our New Year's traditions come from.

- **March**: From Mars, the Roman god of war. This was when armies resumed battle after winter. Even today, March is seen as a month of turbulence and change.

- **May**: From Maia, a Roman fertility goddess. Flowers bloom, crops sprout, and pagans once danced around poles in her honor.

- **June**: From Juno, queen of the Roman gods and protector of marriage. That's why June is still "wedding season."

And then the emperors crowned themselves eternal.

- **July**: Named after Julius Caesar.

- **August**: Named after Augustus Caesar.

The rest? Just numbers in Latin, though they don't line up anymore. "September" means seven, but it's the ninth month. Why? Because the Caesars shoved their names into the middle of the year and broke the count.

Why It Matters

Here's the point: the very structure of modern life—the weeks and months we live by—was shaped by idol worship, mythology, and empire. We don't even notice it. But the Bible never once names days after gods. It simply calls them "the first day… the second day… the seventh day, the Sabbath." God sanctified time differently. He numbered it. He consecrated only one day—the seventh—as holy.

So the question hangs in the air: Whose calendar are you really following? The Most High's, or the Calendar of the gods?

Timeline: From Pagan Gods to Your Calendar

Babylon (c. 2000–500 BC)

- Sun, moon, and stars worshiped as deities.

- Zodiac charts used to order time.

- Festivals aligned with celestial gods.

Ancient Greece (c. 800–300 BC)

- Gods assigned to planets: Ares (Mars), Hermes (Mercury), Zeus (Jupiter), Aphrodite (Venus).

- Lunar calendars tied to Artemis, goddess of the moon.

Rome (c. 100 BC – 400 AD)

- Adopted Greek gods, renamed them: Mars, Mercury, Jupiter, Venus, Saturn.

- 321 AD: Constantine makes *dies Solis* (Sun's Day) the official rest day of the empire.

- Months named after gods and emperors: Janus (January), Mars (March), Maia (May), Juno (June), Julius Caesar (July), Augustus Caesar (August).

Norse & Germanic Tribes (c. 300–700 AD)

- Replaced Roman gods with their own in northern Europe:

  - Tyr → Tuesday

  - Woden (Odin) → Wednesday

  - Thor → Thursday

o Freya → Friday

Medieval Europe (c. 700–1500 AD)

- Latin names for days persist in Catholic lands.

- Germanic/Norse names survive in English-speaking regions.

- Pagan god names blend into Christian calendars.

Modern English (1500s–Today)

- Sunday through Saturday become standard in English.

- January 1 established as New Year's Day (1582, Gregorian Calendar).

- The world adopts Rome's pagan-based calendar system.

*Fast Fact: Every time you check your phone's calendar, you're looking at a direct descendant of the Roman Empire's pagan time system.

Part 2: Birthday Superstitions

Everyone loves a birthday. Balloons, cake, candles, friends singing off-key while the birthday boy or girl squeezes their eyes shut and makes a wish. It feels innocent, even sacred. But where did it all come from?

The truth is, those candles, those cakes, even the act of making a wish, all go back to pagan rituals. That's right—every birthday party you've ever attended is a shadow of ceremonies once offered to gods and goddesses.

Candles, Cakes, and the Moon Goddess

Ancient Greece, fifth century B.C. The people of Athens bring round cakes to the temple of **Artemis**, goddess of the moon and of hunting. The cakes are lit with candles, glowing like the moon she ruled over. Worshipers believed the smoke carried their prayers to Artemis.

Fast-forward to Rome. Families honor their household gods, or *lares*, on birthdays. They place offerings of food and light candles to attract good spirits and ward off the bad ones. The same tradition carried into Germanic paganism, where candles on cakes weren't just decoration—they were spiritual armor, a way to keep away evil forces that supposedly attacked people on the day they were born.

*Did You Know? In pagan belief, birthdays were dangerous. Evil spirits were thought to be especially active, and candles were a way of asking the gods for protection. That's the real reason you still blow them out today.

The Wish

And what about the wish? That's not biblical either. Ancient cultures believed a wish made in silence—without speaking— had magical power. Coupled with the rising smoke of candles, the idea was simple: the gods heard your secret desire and, if pleased, would grant it.

Today, children still close their eyes and "send up" their request. But instead of Artemis or the *lares*, the wish disappears into thin air. The ritual is the same—only the names have changed.

Birthdays in the Bible

Now here's the kicker: in the entire Bible, not one righteous man or woman is recorded celebrating a birthday. Not Abraham, not David, not the prophets, not the apostles, not even Jesus. The only birthday celebrations mentioned belong to pagans and oppressors.

- **Pharaoh's birthday** (Genesis 40:20): he celebrated by executing one of his servants.

- **Herod's birthday** (Matthew 14:6): he celebrated by beheading John the Baptist, one of the greatest prophets of all time.

That's it. Two birthdays. Both tied to death.

Callout: In Scripture, birthdays aren't celebrations of life—they're backdrops for violence.

Meanwhile, Yahweh commanded His people to keep holy days like Passover, the Feast of Weeks, and the Day of Atonement—none of which celebrated personal birth. The focus was always on **God's acts**, not man's.

Why It Matters

Here's what this means: every time we light candles, close our eyes, and make a wish, we're repeating the same patterns used thousands of years ago to honor pagan gods. That means every parent serving cake is unknowingly idol-worshipping. Knowledge of history matters. Traditions matter.

Jesus warned against elevating "the traditions of men" above the commandments of God. And birthdays, as we know them, are exactly that—a tradition of men, with deep pagan roots, dressed up in frosting and sprinkles.

So the next time you blow out candles, ask yourself: Who am I really honoring here?

Timeline: How Birthdays Became Pagan Parties

Ancient Egypt (c. 2500 BC)

- Pharaohs celebrated birthdays as the day of their *deification* (becoming a god).
- Offerings made to the gods, not cakes and balloons.

Ancient Greece (c. 500 BC)

- Worshipers of Artemis offered round, moon-shaped cakes topped with candles.

- Candles symbolized moonlight; smoke carried wishes to the goddess.

Rome (c. 200 BC – 400 AD)

- Families honored *lares* (household gods) on birthdays.

- Offerings and candles meant to protect the birthday person from evil spirits.

- Emperors threw lavish birthday feasts, blending politics with pagan ritual.

Germanic Tribes (c. 500–1000 AD)

- Believed evil spirits targeted people on birthdays.

- Candles on cakes became "spiritual shields."

- Pagan priests introduced the custom of making wishes in silence.

Medieval Europe (c. 1000–1500 AD)

- Catholic tradition absorbed pagan customs.

- Birthday masses blended with old rituals.

- Candles and cake survived under the guise of Christian celebration.

Modern America (1800s–Today)

- German immigrants brought the *Kinderfeste* (children's birthday festival) to the U.S.

- Commercial culture added balloons, parties, and store-bought cakes.

- The old pagan elements—candles, wishes, cakes—remained intact.

Call to Action

History matters. Traditions matter. The next time you're at a birthday party, remember: those candles, those wishes, didn't start with you. They started with gods who aren't real, rituals that God condemned, and traditions designed to pull people's focus off Him.

The question isn't whether you can enjoy life—it's **who gets the glory when you do.**

Questions for Reflection

1. Why do you think the Bible never shows God's people celebrating birthdays, but does record the celebrations of pagan rulers?

2. How do birthday traditions (candles, wishes, parties) shift focus from God's will to human desire?

3. What does Jesus mean when He warns about "the traditions of men" (Mark 7:7–9)?

4. If birthdays were rooted in superstition and idolatry, how might we rethink or reshape the way we celebrate life today?

5. What are better, biblical ways to honor life, family, and milestones without adopting pagan practices?

Part 3: The Grip of Fortune and Luck

Check your morning paper, open a lifestyle app, or scroll Instagram. Chances are, you'll see horoscopes telling you what kind of day you'll have based on the stars. You might even hear someone say, "Cross your fingers," or "Knock on wood." Some people keep a rabbit's foot on a keychain or a horseshoe over their door. They call it harmless. Tradition. Culture.

But here's the truth: every one of these practices has its roots in pagan superstition. What we label "luck" is really the survival of ancient rituals designed to manipulate spirits, summon blessings, or ward off demons.

Horoscopes and Astrology

It starts in **Babylon**, around 2000 B.C. Priests looked to the stars to predict the fate of kings and kingdoms. They created the zodiac—twelve constellations tied to months and seasons. The Greeks and Romans picked it up, naming the zodiac after their gods. To them, your destiny was literally written in the stars.

That system never died. It just changed platforms—from clay tablets to newspapers to apps. People still check horoscopes, still ask which "sign" they are, still believe Mars or Venus affects their love life.

Did You Know? The prophet Isaiah mocked astrologers in his day: *"Let now the astrologers, the stargazers… stand up, and save thee from these things that shall come upon thee"* (Isaiah 47:13). His point? They couldn't.

Charms and Lucky Objects

The **rabbit's foot**? Celtic tribes believed rabbits were sacred to fertility gods because of their breeding power. Carrying a piece of one supposedly transferred that fertility and fortune to you.

The **horseshoe**? That comes from worship of the crescent moon, tied to goddesses of fertility and harvest. Hung over a doorway, it was thought to draw in blessing and repel evil.

The **four-leaf clover**? A Druid symbol. Finding one was seen as a magical sign of favor from nature spirits.

Callout: When people say "Good luck," they're echoing ancient invocations to Fortuna, the Roman goddess of chance.

Knocking on Wood

Ever tap a table or doorframe to "avoid bad luck"? That's not random. Ancient Celts believed spirits and gods lived inside trees. Knocking on wood summoned their protection—or kept them from hearing your boast and turning against you.

Even today, when people say something good and then rap their knuckles on a desk, they're reenacting the same ritual from thousands of years ago.

Crossing Fingers

This one comes from **pagan Europe**. The idea was that two people crossing fingers created a "concentration point" for good spirits. Later, Christians adapted it into a hidden sign of the cross during times of persecution. Today, kids say "fingers crossed" for good luck, not realizing they're practicing a ritual rooted in superstition.

Why It Matters

Here's the reality: none of these customs are neutral. They teach people to trust in objects, gestures, or cosmic forces instead of the living God. That's idolatry in disguise. The Bible says plainly:

- *"Learn not the way of the heathen... be not dismayed at the signs of heaven"* (Jeremiah 10:2).

- *"Blessed is the man that trusteth in the LORD"* (Jeremiah 17:7).

So when we cross our fingers, knock on wood, or check our horoscope, we're not just being cute—we're leaning on the same pagan systems God warned His people to avoid.

And the question is simple: do you want luck, or do you want the blessing of the Most High?

Call to Action

The next time someone says, "Good luck," flip it. Say, "God bless." When you're tempted to check a horoscope or grab a charm, stop. Ask yourself: *Am I calling on fortune, or am I calling on the Lord?*

Questions for Reflection

1. Why do you think people are still drawn to horoscopes and charms, even in an age of science and reason?

2. Have you ever relied on "luck" instead of prayer? What happened?

3. How does superstition undermine faith in God's promises?

4. What's the difference between trusting in "chance" and trusting in God's sovereignty?

Chapter 2
Paganism in our Celebrations

Holidays are the one time of year people will do the strangest things without asking a single question. Think about it: we chop down a tree, drag it into the living room, hang socks on the fireplace, and then tell kids a bearded man breaks into the house at midnight but—don't worry—he's friendly. In April, we hand kids plastic eggs laid by a rabbit, even though rabbits don't lay eggs, and nobody blinks. Come October, we dress our kids as zombies and send them to strangers' doors demanding candy with the threat of violence built right into the greeting: "Trick or treat!" And we call this wholesome family fun.

Then there's New Year's Eve. Millions of adults gather in freezing weather to watch a glowing ball fall down a pole while counting backward like toddlers learning numbers. At Thanksgiving, we slaughter turkeys by the millions while pretending it's about gratitude, not gluttony. Valentine's Day? People spend billions on chocolate and roses to prove love in 24 hours flat—because apparently affection expires if not renewed annually. The truth is, our holidays make no sense at all—unless you remember where they came from. Then you realize: the gods are still laughing.

Part 1: The Pagan Holidays We Keep

Look at a modern calendar. It's full of red-letter days: Christmas, Easter, Halloween, New Year's. They're the biggest celebrations in the Western world. Billions of people take part—decorating trees, painting eggs, carving pumpkins, clinking champagne glasses. But here's the question nobody asks: **where did these traditions come from?**

The truth is stark. None of these holidays originated in the Bible. Every single one has **pagan roots**—rituals designed for the gods, not God. And while churches and culture have baptized them in new names, the foundations remain the same.

Christmas: The Birthday of the Sun

December 25. For most Christians, it's the birthday of Jesus. But the Bible never gives a date for His birth—and certainly not in winter. So why December 25?

Rome, 274 A.D. Emperor Aurelian declares December 25th the *Dies Natalis Solis Invicti*—the birthday of the "Unconquered Sun." Pagan worshipers celebrated the sun's return after the winter solstice, with fire, feasting, and gift-giving. When Christianity spread through Rome, the date was recycled: instead of honoring the sun, it was now honoring the Son.

But the symbols didn't change. The **evergreen tree**? A fertility idol in Norse and Germanic tradition, representing life that never dies. The **Yule log**? A burnt offering to pagan gods during the twelve days of Yule. The **mistletoe**? Sacred to Druids, used in fertility rituals.

*Did You Know?** Jeremiah 10:2–4 warns against cutting a tree, decorating it with silver and gold, and fastening it upright. Sounds eerily like a Christmas tree.

Easter: The Fertility Feast

The very name "Easter" doesn't come from the Bible. It comes from **Ishtar**, the Babylonian goddess of love and fertility. Her spring festival was filled with symbols of new life—eggs, rabbits, and sunrise worship.

In the second century, Christians in Rome blended the resurrection of Christ with the old fertility festival. The egg became a symbol of new life; the rabbit, of endless fertility. The sunrise service? That comes straight from ancient sun worship, greeting the dawn with prayers. The true crucifixion and resurrection of Jesus are celebrated during the Passover and Feast of First Fruits High Holy days.

Callout: Ezekiel 8:16 records God's people committing abomination by turning their backs on the temple of God and facing east to worship the sun at dawn. Today, millions reenact the same act at Easter sunrise services.

Halloween: Night of the Spirits

October 31. Kids dress as witches, skeletons, and superheroes. They roam door-to-door shouting "Trick or treat!" It feels like innocent fun. But its origins are anything but.

The ancient Celts called it **Samhain** (pronounced sow-in), the night when the veil between the living and the dead was thinnest. Druids lit bonfires, wore masks to ward off spirits, and left food to appease wandering souls.

The Catholic Church tried to Christianize it by declaring November 1 "All Saints' Day" and October 31 "All Hallows' Eve." But the costumes, the candy, the obsession with death? Those are straight out of Druidic superstition.

Did You Know? "Trick or treat" comes from the old belief that spirits would curse your home if not appeased with offerings.

New Year's Day: The Two-Faced God

January 1 is the most celebrated date in the world. Fireworks, countdowns, champagne toasts—it feels universal. But like the rest, it's pagan.

The month of **January** is named after **Janus**, the Roman two-faced god of beginnings and transitions. One face looked forward, the other back. Romans honored him on January 1 with sacrifices and vows for the new year. Sound familiar? That's the origin of your New Year's resolutions.

The champagne toast, too, isn't random. Pouring out wine and drinking to health was an ancient libation ritual, an offering to the gods before consuming it yourself.

Callout: While the Bible marks the beginning of the year in the spring (Exodus 12:2), Rome moved it to winter to honor Janus. The whole system is man-made.

Valentine's Day: From Fertility to Cupid's Arrow

Every February 14, millions of couples exchange cards, flowers, and chocolates. Cupid decorates store shelves as the symbol of love. But the roots of Valentine's Day aren't romantic—they're pagan.

In ancient Rome, February was the month of purification and fertility. The **Festival of Lupercalia** (February 13–15) honored Lupercus, a fertility god. Priests sacrificed goats and dogs, then smeared the blood on young men. They ran through the streets, striking women with goat hides to promote fertility.

Later, the Catholic Church tried to Christianize the day by tying it to "St. Valentine." But the old rituals lingered—especially Cupid, originally the Roman god of desire, armed with his magical arrows.

*Did You Know? The heart symbol, so common on Valentine's Day, comes from an ancient pagan depiction of the female form associated with fertility.

Mother's Day & Father's Day: Pagan Roots of Family Festivals

Celebrating parents sounds innocent. But the first "Mother's Day" festivals honored goddesses, not moms. The Greeks held festivals for **Rhea**, mother of the gods. Romans worshiped **Cybele** with processions and sacrifices. Both were tied to fertility cults.

Modern Mother's Day was formalized in the U.S. in 1914, pushed by Anna Jarvis—but it borrowed the language and imagery of those earlier goddess festivals.

Father's Day has similar baggage. In Catholic Europe, March 19 honored **Saint Joseph**. But older traditions included celebrations of male fertility gods and patriarchal household spirits.

Callout: Honoring parents is a commandment (Exodus 20:12). But dedicating entire holy days rooted in goddess and fertility worship? That's man's invention.

Thanksgiving: The Sacrificial Feast

Every November, Americans gather to eat turkey, stuffing, and pie in the name of gratitude. The official story says Pilgrims and Native Americans shared a peaceful meal in 1621. The reality is darker.

For many Native tribes, Thanksgiving marks the beginning of dispossession and slaughter. The "sacred bird" for many indigenous peoples—the turkey—was killed and consumed en masse, stripped of its spiritual meaning. Later Thanksgivings were declared after colonial victories over Native tribes, effectively turning the meal into a celebration of conquest.

Even the cornucopia, a common Thanksgiving symbol, comes from **Greek mythology**—the horn of Amalthea, a goat that nourished Zeus. It became a pagan emblem of abundance and harvest.

Did You Know? In 1637, Massachusetts declared a "Thanksgiving" after colonists massacred 700 Pequot men, women, and children. For many Native Americans, that's the real history behind the holiday.

Why It Matters

So here's the bottom line: the biggest holidays on the planet are not neutral. They're ancient pagan festivals, repackaged with Christian names and modern flair.

- Christmas celebrates the **sun god**, not Christ.

- Easter is tied to **Ishtar**, not the resurrection.

- Halloween comes from **Samhain**, not Scripture.

- New Year's Day honors **Janus**, not the God of Israel.

Jesus said, *"In vain do they worship me, teaching for doctrines the commandments of men"* (Mark 7:7). These holidays are the very definition of man-made commandments—designed to please culture, not God.

The question is simple: are we worshiping the Creator on His terms, or are we still bowing to the gods of Rome, Babylon, and the Druids without realizing it?

Call to Action

You can't change the past, but you can change what you do today. Stop calling paganism by another name. If you want to honor God, keep His appointed times, not man's imitations.

Questions for Reflection

1. Why do you think these pagan holidays were absorbed into Western culture so completely?

2. How do symbols like trees, eggs, and rabbits affect the way people view God's truth?

3. What are some dangers of mixing biblical worship with pagan traditions?

4. How does keeping God's feasts (Sabbath, Passover, etc.) provide a different, biblical alternative?

Part 2: The True Biblical Holidays

We've seen how modern holidays—Christmas, Easter, Halloween, Valentine's Day—are built on pagan foundations. But God gave His people a different set of days. Not man-made, not borrowed from Babylon or Rome, but straight from His own mouth.

Leviticus 23 calls them the **Feasts of the LORD**. They aren't "Jewish holidays." They're God's appointed times—prophetic rehearsals of His plan of salvation. And here's the shocker: every single one points directly to **Jesus Christ (Yahusha the Messiah).** He himself kept all of them when he walked the earth. In Exodus 12:14 God is very clear; we must keep these feasts forever! "And this day shall be unto you for a memorial; and ye shall keep it a feast to Yahweh throughout your generations; ye shall keep it a feast by an ordinance for ever."

The Weekly Sabbath (Shabbat)

- **Command:** "Remember the Sabbath day, to keep it holy" (Exodus 20:8).

- **Meaning:** A day of rest, set apart since creation (Genesis 2:2–3).

- **Fulfillment in Christ:** Jesus is the **Lord of the Sabbath** (Mark 2:27–28). In Him we find true rest (Hebrews 4:9–10).

- **Jesus Kept the Sabbath:** "And he came to Nazareth, where he had been brought up: and, as his custom was, he went into the synagogue on the sabbath day, and stood up for to read." Luke 4:16

- **Apostle Paul kept the Sabbath:** "And Paul, as his manner was, went in unto them, and three sabbath day reasoned with them out of the scriptures" Acts 17:2

Did You Know? The Sabbath is the only day God personally blessed and sanctified before sin even entered the world.

Passover (Pesach)

- **Command:** Commemorate Israel's deliverance from Egypt by the blood of the lamb (Exodus 12:1–14).

- **Fulfillment in Christ:** Jesus is the **Lamb of God** (John 1:29). He was crucified at Passover, His blood covering sin once for all (1 Corinthians 5:7).

Callout: When the angel of death "passed over" Israel, it foreshadowed the cross—where death passes over all who are under Christ's blood.

- Jesus celebrated the Passover at the Last Supper and would become our Passover Lamb.

Feast of Unleavened Bread

- **Command:** Seven days of eating bread without leaven, symbolizing removal of sin (Exodus 12:15–20).

- **Fulfillment in Christ:** Jesus' **sinless body** lay in the tomb during this feast. Believers are called to live "unleavened," free from sin (1 Corinthians 5:8).

Firstfruits

- **Command:** Offer the first sheaf of the barley harvest to the LORD (Leviticus 23:9–14).

- **Fulfillment in Christ:** Jesus rose on **Firstfruits**, becoming the **firstborn from the dead** (1 Corinthians 15:20). His resurrection guarantees ours.

- The important High Holy day of Firstfruits celebrates Jesus' resurrection.

Pentecost (Shavuot)

- **Command:** Count 50 days from Firstfruits, then offer the firstfruits of the wheat harvest (Leviticus 23:15–21).

- **Fulfillment in Christ:** On this day the **Holy Spirit was poured out** (Acts 2), writing God's law on hearts instead of stone (Jeremiah 31:33).

Feast of Trumpets (Yom Teruah)

- **Command:** A memorial of trumpet blasts on the first day of the seventh month (Leviticus 23:23–25).

- **Fulfillment in Christ:** Symbolic of His **second coming**, announced with the trumpet of God (1 Thessalonians 4:16; Matthew 24:31).

Did You Know? The "last trumpet" Paul speaks of (1 Corinthians 15:52) connects directly to this feast.

Day of Atonement (Yom Kippur)

- **Command:** A day of fasting, repentance, and priestly atonement for Israel (Leviticus 16; 23:26–32).

- **Fulfillment in Christ:** Jesus is our **High Priest**, entering heaven with His own blood (Hebrews 9:11–12). His sacrifice atones once for all (Hebrews 10:10–14).

- On this day we fast, pray, and repent for all the sins we committed over the past year while receiving cleansing from the blood of Jesus.

Feast of Tabernacles (Sukkot)

- **Command:** Dwell in booths seven days, remembering God's presence in the wilderness (Leviticus 23:33–43).

- **Fulfillment in Christ:** Jesus **tabernacled among us** (John 1:14). This feast looks forward to God dwelling with His people forever (Revelation 21:3).

- Tabernacles is often celebrated with a camping trip as we move out of the comforts of home into the wilderness to trust Yahweh alone.

The Eighth Day (Shemini Atzeret)

- **Command:** A solemn assembly at the close of Tabernacles (Leviticus 23:36, 39).

- **Fulfillment in Christ:** Foreshadows the **new creation**, the eternal rest beyond this world (Revelation 21:1–5).

Why It Matters

Here's the difference:

- Pagan holidays celebrate fertility gods, sun gods, and conquest.

- God's holy days celebrate **deliverance, resurrection, atonement, and eternal life.**

Every biblical feast is Christ-centered prophecy. The spring feasts (Passover through Pentecost) point to His first coming. The fall feasts (Trumpets through Tabernacles) point to His return.

These aren't empty rituals. They're God's calendar—His roadmap of redemption. And they put the spotlight where it belongs: not on tradition, not on man, but on Christ.

Call to Action

The world runs on the Calendar of the Gods. But God gave us a better one—His. The invitation is clear: step off the hamster wheel of man-made holidays and step into the prophetic rhythm of God's appointed times.

Brothers and sisters, hear me today: when the Body of Christ clings to pagan rituals, it robs itself of power. The world says decorate a tree, hide eggs, bow to man-made traditions — but the Word says, *"Learn not the way of the heathen"* (Jeremiah 10:2). Jesus warned, *"In vain do they worship me, teaching for doctrines the commandments of men"* (Mark 7:7). Every time the church celebrates what God never commanded, it blurs the line between holy and profane. That confusion weakens our testimony, divides our fellowship, and keeps us from walking in the fullness of the Spirit. A compromised church cannot be a conquering church.

But there is a better way — the way of the Lord's appointed times. God Himself laid out His Feasts in Leviticus 23, and every one points to Christ. Passover reveals His sacrifice, Firstfruits His resurrection, Pentecost His Spirit, Trumpets His return, Atonement His cleansing, Tabernacles His dwelling with us forever. Paul declares in Ephesians 2:12–14 that through Christ we are grafted into the **commonwealth of Israel** — one body, one covenant, one people. When we keep the Lord's Feasts, we step onto His calendar and into His promises. This strengthens the Body, unites believers in truth, and makes us a powerful witness in a world drowning in lies. Church, it's time to lay down the traditions of men and rise up in the appointed times of God!

Questions for Reflection

1. Why do you think God gave His people appointed times instead of leaving worship up to culture?

2. How does seeing Christ in the feasts change the way you view the Old Testament?

3. What might happen if believers today returned to celebrating God's feasts instead of pagan holidays?

Chapter 3
Part III: Paganism in Family Rituals

Part 1: Marriage Paganized

Weddings are supposed to be sacred. Two people standing before God, vowing faithfulness, becoming one flesh. That's biblical. But the way we celebrate weddings today? Rings, veils, bouquets, rice showers—it's a circus of rituals most people don't realize come straight out of paganism. What was once a holy covenant has been buried under layers of superstition and tradition.

Weddings might be the only place where grown adults willingly spend thousands of dollars reenacting ancient superstitions without a second thought. We put rings on fingers because Romans thought it meant ownership, throw rice in the air like it's fertilizer, and force brides to carry flowers because someone once believed garlic scared away evil spirits. Then there's the veil — once a pagan invisibility cloak for demons, now an overpriced piece of lace that blocks the bride's vision until someone lifts it at just the right moment. It's less "holy covenant" and more "costume party with contracts."

And don't forget the bouquet toss. Nothing says "eternal love" like launching a bundle of flowers into a mob of single women desperate enough to risk sprained ankles for a shot at being next in line. Meanwhile, the groom gets to toss a sweaty piece of clothing into the same crowd — a tradition that would get you arrested if you tried it anywhere else. Add in the DJ yelling, "Everybody clap your hands!" and suddenly the most sacred covenant God ever created looks suspiciously like a Vegas floor show.

The Ring: A Circle with Pagan Roots

Slip a ring on a finger and everyone calls it holy matrimony. But the practice didn't start with Scripture—it started in pagan Rome and Egypt. Egyptians believed a circle symbolized eternity, and the hole in the middle was a gateway to the unknown. Romans used rings as **contracts of ownership**, not love. The ring was a seal: "This woman is mine."

Did You Know? The so-called "vein of love" connecting the fourth finger to the heart is a Roman myth, not science—and certainly not Bible.

The Veil: Hiding from Spirits

That white veil looks pure, but its origin isn't innocence—it's fear. In ancient Rome and Greece, brides wore veils to hide from jealous spirits who might try to harm them. In some cultures, veils symbolized submission to fertility gods. The church baptized it as "modesty," but the roots remain pagan.

The Bouquet: More Than Flowers

Why do brides carry flowers? Not for beauty. Ancient Greeks and Romans gave brides **herbs and garlic** to ward off evil spirits. Later, it became fertility symbols: flowers representing fruitfulness, blossoms symbolizing new life. Today it's just decoration—but the history is steeped in superstition.

And tossing the bouquet? That came from medieval Europe, where catching a piece of the bride's clothing was thought to transfer luck and fertility. Flowers replaced torn dresses, but the idea stayed the same.

The Rice Toss: Fertility from the Sky

Showering a couple with rice—or confetti, birdseed, or petals—goes back to pagan fertility rites. The act symbolized showering the couple with the seed of prosperity and many children. In other words, it was magic, not blessing.

Callout: The Bible says children are a heritage from the LORD (Psalm 127:3), not from rice or petals tossed in the air.

The Roman Contract

The Bible defines marriage as a covenant (Genesis 2:24). But Rome turned it into a contract. A man gave a token (often a ring) as proof of ownership. Families exchanged dowries. Priests of pagan temples presided. The ritual was less about covenant before God and more about property, fertility, and social order.

The sad truth? Much of today's wedding ceremony is just that Roman model dressed up in lace and white dresses.

Why It Matters

Marriage is supposed to be holy, a picture of Christ and the church (Ephesians 5:31–32). But when we smuggle in veils to hide from spirits, rings rooted in ownership contracts, bouquets tied to fertility gods, and rice as magic seed—we dilute the covenant God designed. What God created as pure has been polluted by pagan traditions.

The covenant is still holy. The vows still matter. But we must be honest: the rituals we cling to aren't from Scripture. They're leftovers from idolatry. And that matters because truth matters.

Call to Action

The rituals of man may look beautiful, but they can't sanctify a marriage. What makes marriage holy is the covenant, the vows, and the presence of God. The challenge is clear: strip away the superstition, keep the covenant pure, and let the wedding point not to Rome's traditions, but to Christ and His church.

Questions for Reflection

1. How does knowing the pagan roots of common wedding traditions change the way you view them?

2. Do rings, veils, bouquets, and rice point us toward God's covenant—or toward superstition?

3. What does Scripture emphasize about marriage that culture often ignores?

4. How can believers reclaim the wedding ceremony as a true **covenant before God**, rather than a show of traditions?

5. If marriage is meant to mirror Christ and His church (Ephesians 5:31–32), what elements should be central in a biblical wedding?

Part 2: Funerals, Ancestors, and Spirits of the Dead

Beloved, funerals are not the end of the story. The world has turned them into ceremonies filled with superstition—libations for the dead, prayers to ancestors, rituals to "guide souls." But the Word of God says plainly, *"The dead know not any thing"* (Ecclesiastes 9:5). Our hope is not in candles, charms, or chants. Our hope is in Christ, who declared, *"I am the resurrection and the life: he that believeth in me, though he were dead, yet shall he live"* (John 11:25). Pagan rituals leave people in fear of spirits. The gospel leaves us in faith in the Savior.

Funerals should not be moments of confusion but of clarity. We don't gather to feed spirits or negotiate with ancestors. We gather to honor the life of the departed and to remind the living that Christ has conquered the grave. *"O death, where is thy sting? O grave, where is thy victory?"* (1 Corinthians 15:55). The sting is gone because Jesus bore it at the cross. The victory is ours because He walked out of the tomb. That's why our funerals should not echo the darkness of the nations, but shine with the light of resurrection hope.

Funerals are meant to honor the dead and comfort the living. But look closely, and you'll see that much of what we do at funerals has little to do with the Bible and everything to do with pagan rituals. From pouring out drinks for the dead, to praying for souls in the afterlife, to elaborate wakes and ancestor veneration—these practices come straight from ancient superstition, not Scripture.

Libations: Pouring One Out

Maybe you've seen it—someone tilts a bottle and pours a little on the ground "for the homies." That's not new. It's a practice thousands of years old. The Egyptians poured wine for Osiris, the Greeks for Zeus, the Romans for their household gods. The belief was simple: the spirits of the dead needed drink offerings to stay appeased in the afterlife. Today, people repeat the same ritual without realizing they're echoing pagan worship.

*Did You Know? Paul warned the Corinthians about this exact thing: *"The things which the Gentiles sacrifice, they sacrifice to devils, and not to God"* (1 Corinthians 10:20).

Wakes and Vigils

The all-night vigil—what we call a "wake"—originated with the Celts. They believed spirits wandered between worlds after death, so family members sat watch to protect the body and keep evil away. Food and drink were offered to the spirit of the deceased, a practice still alive in some cultures today.

Contrast that with Scripture: the Bible says plainly, *"The dead know not any thing"* (Ecclesiastes 9:5). God's people never kept watch to feed or protect a wandering soul—because there was no wandering soul.

Ancestor Worship

In Africa, Asia, and the Americas, many cultures elevated the dead into guardians of the living. Food, incense, and prayers were offered to grandparents and forefathers. Rome had the *lares*—household spirits thought to guide families. The idea survives in subtle ways today: prayers for the dead, lighting candles for departed loved ones, or believing ancestors intercede for us.

But the Bible draws a hard line: *"There shall not be found among you... a consulter with familiar spirits, or a necromancer"* (Deuteronomy 18:10–11). Communication with the dead is strictly forbidden.

Catholic "Purgatory"

The doctrine of purgatory, where souls are supposedly purified by prayers and masses, isn't in the Bible. It's a direct borrowing from pagan ancestor veneration, where the living were thought to influence the destiny of the dead. Scripture says the opposite: *"It is appointed unto men once to die, but after this the judgment"* (Hebrews 9:27). No second chances, no prayers to change someone's fate.

Why It Matters

God's Word is clear: death is not the end, but the dead are asleep until the resurrection. Pagan funeral rituals—libations, vigils, prayers for the dead—confuse that truth. They keep people bound in fear and superstition instead of hope. Jesus said, *"I am the resurrection and the life: he that believeth in me, though he were dead, yet shall he live"* (John 11:25). That's the comfort of Scripture.

Funerals should point to Christ, not to spirits. Hope, not superstition. Resurrection, not rituals. Anything less weakens faith and drags the living into the darkness of pagan lies.

Hope Beyond the Grave

Theme Verse: *"I am the resurrection, and the life: he that believeth in me, though he were dead, yet shall he live."* — John 11:25

1. Death Is Not the End — It's a Sleep

- *Ecclesiastes 9:5* — "The dead know not any thing."

- *1 Thessalonians 4:13–14* — Believers "sleep in Jesus" until the resurrection.

- Death in Scripture is a temporary pause, not eternal wandering of spirits.

Key Point: The world fears death; God calls it sleep.

2. Pagan Traditions Distort the Truth

- Libations, ancestor worship, and prayers for the dead come from Egypt, Rome, and Druid rituals.

- *Deuteronomy 18:10–11* forbids communication with the dead.

- *1 Corinthians 10:20* warns sacrifices to idols are sacrifices to demons.

Key Point: We don't honor the dead with superstition—we honor them by trusting God's Word.

3. Christ Conquered the Grave

- *1 Corinthians 15:55* — "O death, where is thy sting? O grave, where is thy victory?"

- *Hebrews 2:14–15* — Jesus destroyed the one who held the power of death.

- The cross and resurrection broke the chains of fear.

Key Point: Death is defeated; the grave has no claim on those in Christ.

4. The Resurrection Is Our Blessed Hope

- *1 Thessalonians 4:16–17* — At the trumpet, the dead in Christ rise first.

- *Revelation 21:4* — God will wipe away every tear; death will be no more.

- Funerals are not final chapters—they point forward to the day of reunion and glory.

Key Point: We bury in sorrow, but we rise in victory.

Funerals are not about fear, but faith. Not about spirits, but about the Spirit. Not about the finality of death, but the certainty of resurrection. Let us leave behind the traditions of men and hold fast to the promise of Christ: *"Because I live, ye shall live also"* (John 14:19).

Questions for Reflection

1. How does Scripture's teaching that the dead "sleep" until resurrection differ from common cultural beliefs about death?

2. Why do you think so many cultures developed rituals of ancestor veneration and offerings for the dead?

3. What dangers exist when we mix funeral practices with pagan superstitions?

4. How does Christ's resurrection reshape the way believers approach funerals?

5. If funerals are meant to comfort the living, what truths from Scripture can we emphasize instead of empty traditions?

6. How can we honor the dead in ways that strengthen faith in God rather than superstition?

Part 3: Children and Pagan Play

The Tooth Fairy: Tiny Spirit, Big Lie

Picture this: a kid loses a tooth. Instead of telling him it's part of growing up, we sneak into his room in the middle of the night, slip a dollar under his pillow, and then lie about a winged fairy who apparently breaks and enters for dental work. Imagine explaining that to one of the ancient Israelite prophets: "Yes Jeremiah, we tell our children that magical fairies collect human teeth as currency, but it's totally normal." If that's not weird enough, adults are the ones carrying out the con— leaving kids to believe the Tooth Fairy is somewhere out there running a black market of molars.

On the surface, the Tooth Fairy seems like harmless fun. A child loses a tooth, and overnight it's transformed into money. But where did this idea come from? In ancient Europe, people believed teeth contained magical power. Vikings kept children's teeth as good luck charms in battle. Other cultures buried or burned baby teeth to keep witches from using them in spells. The modern "fairy" was simply a sweet cover for a very old superstition about spirits collecting body parts.

Did You Know? In Norse mythology, there were *álfar*—tooth-collecting elves who supposedly gave blessings in return. The Tooth Fairy is their PR makeover.

And here's the kicker: parents don't just tolerate this—they fund it. Adults act like covert agents, sneaking into bedrooms at midnight to swap teeth for cash. If you did that outside your house, it would be breaking and entering. Inside your house, it's "tradition."

Santa Claus: The All-Seeing Father Christmas

Then we get to Santa. Everyone knows the jolly old man with reindeer, sleigh bells, and a bottomless bag of toys. But dig deeper, and you'll find a mash-up of pagan gods.

- **Odin**, the Norse chief god, rode through the skies on an eight-legged horse, watching children and rewarding or punishing them. Sound familiar? Santa traded the horse for reindeer.

- **Saturn**, the Roman god celebrated during Saturnalia, was honored with gift-giving and feasts in December.

- Later, the Catholic Church overlaid this with *Saint Nicholas*, known for gift-giving. Combine Odin, Saturn, and Nicholas, wrap it in Coca-Cola marketing, and you've got Santa.

Callout: Parents tell kids Santa sees them "when they're sleeping" and "knows when they're awake." In other words, he's omniscient—a role that belongs only to God.

Meanwhile, children learn to write letters to Santa, not prayers to the Lord. They learn obedience for gifts, not holiness for Christ. And we wonder why the real meaning of Christmas is lost.

The Easter Bunny: Fertility in Disguise

Finally, there's the Easter Bunny. No matter how you dress it up, it makes zero sense: rabbits don't lay eggs. But in pagan fertility cults, it made perfect sense.

- Rabbits symbolized fertility because of their rapid breeding.

- Eggs symbolized new life and reproduction.

- Together, they were sacred to **Ishtar** (Babylonian goddess of fertility) and **Eostre** (Germanic goddess of spring).

When Christianity spread through Europe, the church overlayed these fertility rituals into Resurrection Sunday. But instead of pointing to the risen Christ, children ended up focused on egg hunts and chocolate bunnies.

Did You Know? Ezekiel 8:16 condemns Israel for turning their backs on the temple to face the rising sun—exactly the kind of sunrise rituals tied to Easter traditions.

Why It Matters

Here's the truth: these "children's traditions" aren't neutral fun. They're training exercises in pagan superstition. They teach kids to believe in magical beings that see all, reward or punish, and trade in offerings. Instead of pointing children to the God of Scripture, parents fill their imagination with fables—and then wonder why faith feels like just another story when they grow up.

Paul warned Timothy: *"They shall turn away their ears from the truth, and shall be turned unto fables"* (2 Timothy 4:4). That's exactly what these childhood traditions are: fables. And unless we pull them down, they'll keep shaping the next generation.

Call to Action

Children are a heritage from the LORD (Psalm 127:3). They don't need fables to make life magical—they need the truth to make life meaningful. Parents and teachers have a choice: pass down pagan traditions, or pass down the Word of God. One path leads to confusion. The other leads to Christ.

Questions for Reflection

1. How do these traditions (Tooth Fairy, Santa, Easter Bunny) shape the way children think about truth and faith?

2. Why is it dangerous to let children grow up trusting fables more than Scripture?

3. What are some ways parents can celebrate milestones and holidays without turning to pagan superstitions?

4. How can families redirect children's focus to God's appointed times and biblical truths?

5. What long-term effect might it have on a child's faith if they learn early that parents lied about Santa or the Tooth Fairy?

Chapter 4
Paganism in Modern Culture

Part 1: Pop Culture's Pagan Heroes

Imagine explaining modern movies to someone from the first century. You'd sit down a Roman soldier and say, "So, here's the deal. Two thousand years from now, kids will line up to watch Thor—yes, *your Thor*—on the big screen. Only now he's got perfect hair, a magic hammer, and he cracks jokes while saving the universe." The soldier would probably choke on his wine. Back then, people offered goats and prayers to Thor. Today, we offer $12 at the box office and a bucket of popcorn.

It doesn't stop there. Zeus, once the mighty sky god of Olympus, now stars in Disney cartoons. Loki, the trickster who caused fear in Norse sagas, has his own fan club. The Egyptians worshiped Anubis as lord of the dead; now he's a video game character with a weapon upgrade. Even the Mayan gods, once fed with blood sacrifices, show up as collectible trading cards. Somewhere in the afterlife, these idols must be blushing—or laughing—that humanity still can't quit them.

And of course, Marvel and DC keep the machine going. Odin, Thor, Hercules, Ares—all get screen time, merchandising, and action figures. Kids wear T-shirts with gods their ancestors once feared. Adults cheer for Zeus as if he were a misunderstood grandfather with lightning issues. The modern world doesn't bow in temples—it bows in theaters. Different altars, same gods.

Thor: From Norse God to Marvel Superstar

Thor wasn't born in a comic book. He was worshiped by the Norse as the hammer-wielding god of thunder, fertility, and war. Vikings prayed to him before battle, sacrificed to him for harvests, and wore hammer amulets to invoke his power. The day Thursday is literally "Thor's Day."

Fast-forward to today. Hollywood has cleaned him up, slapped him in a cape, and turned him into a charming Avenger. People no longer chant hymns to Thor—they buy tickets to watch him smash aliens. But the net effect is the same: a pagan god still commands attention, influence, and loyalty.

Did You Know? The Norse believed Thor rode through the sky in a chariot pulled by goats. Marvel swapped the goats for CGI lightning, but the myth is the same.

Zeus: King of the Gods, King of the Screens

In Greek mythology, Zeus was the supreme ruler of Olympus, feared for his lightning and infamous for chasing women.

Ancient Greeks offered sacrifices at his temples, believing he controlled rain, storms, and justice.

Today, Zeus shows up in cartoons, video games, and blockbuster movies. He's often softened into a wise old mentor, but the core is unchanged: he's still portrayed as a powerful ruler of heaven. Kids grow up knowing Zeus's name but not God's Word. That's not an accident—it's culture keeping idolatry alive under the banner of "mythology."

Anubis: From Death God to Digital Icon

The Egyptians feared Anubis, the jackal-headed god of the afterlife. Priests called on him during mummification, believing he weighed the souls of the dead. Entire cults formed around appeasing him.

Now? Anubis is a favorite in video games, complete with glowing eyes and mystical powers. Instead of priests, gamers channel his image through consoles and screens. What was once worshiped in tombs is now worshiped in pixels. Different temple, same devotion.

Loki and the Trickster Cult

The Norse trickster god Loki caused chaos wherever he went. He was feared, not loved. But modern pop culture has recast him as a fan favorite—sarcastic, misunderstood, even likable. Millions binge-watch shows about him, wear his merch, and defend his character arcs.

The result? A god once blamed for disaster is now idolized as a clever antihero. The devil himself couldn't design a better PR campaign.

Why It Matters

Here's the point: ancient idols didn't die—they just got repackaged. Hollywood, comics, video games—they've resurrected pagan gods for a modern audience. And instead of temples, the new altars are theaters, streaming services, and merchandise shelves.

The Bible warns, *"What the Gentiles sacrifice, they sacrifice to devils, and not to God"* (1 Corinthians 10:20). Behind every idol is a demonic influence, whether it's a golden statue or a Marvel superhero. When we cheer for Thor, laugh with Loki, or admire Zeus, we're not just watching entertainment—we're normalizing idolatry.

Different names. Different platforms. Same deception.

Call to Action

You may not bow at Thor's altar or bring offerings to Zeus, but every time you give your time, money, and imagination to these idols, you're feeding the same spirits that demanded worship thousands of years ago. Remember the words of Joshua: *"Choose you this day whom ye will serve"* (Joshua 24:15). Entertainment is never neutral—make sure it strengthens your walk with Christ instead of pulling you back toward idols in disguise.

Questions for Reflection

1. Why do you think pagan gods are so popular in movies, shows, and games today?

2. How does pop culture's "mythology" normalize idolatry in a way that feels harmless?

3. Are there shows, movies, or games you enjoy that might be shaping your view of good and evil without you realizing it?

4. What's the difference between learning mythology as history and consuming it as entertainment?

5. How can we engage with culture without letting pagan idols take root in our hearts and homes?

Part 2: Music, Magic, and Mysticism

Beloved, let me tell you something straight: music is powerful. From the beginning of time, songs have carried spirits. David's harp drove demons out of Saul (1 Samuel 16:23). And today, the devil knows the same truth—music can move you, shape you, and chain you. That's why so much of modern music is filled with chants, spells, and images that don't glorify God, but glorify darkness.

Look at the culture: young people walking around with earbuds in, filling their minds with songs about death, sex, rebellion, and the occult. You don't have to be a prophet to see what's happening—the enemy is discipling a generation through a beat. He doesn't need a pulpit when he's got Spotify. He doesn't need an altar when he's got the stage. Lyrics become sermons, and concerts become worship services for idols in disguise.

And make no mistake—this isn't harmless. From tarot cards on album covers to Ouija boards in music videos, from artists bragging about selling their soul to satanic symbols flashing at halftime shows, the evidence is right in front of us. The devil has always wanted worship (Matthew 4:9), and now he's getting it through the playlists of millions. The question is not *whether* music shapes you. The question is: which spirit is shaping you?

Tarot Cards and Occult Imagery

Flip through music videos today and you'll see tarot cards everywhere. They aren't props—they're pagan tools. The tarot deck came from 15th-century Europe, adapted from even older occult systems. Each card represents spirits, fate, and destiny. Musicians flash them because they know the symbolism resonates with mysticism. Whether it's the "Death" card in a rap video or "The Lovers" card in a pop performance, the message is the same: trust the cards, not the Creator.

Did You Know? Deuteronomy 18:10–12 strictly forbids divination and calling on spirits. Tarot isn't entertainment—it's rebellion against God.

The Ouija Board and Spirit Games

It started in the 1800s as a parlor game, but the Ouija board has always been tied to necromancy—contacting the dead. In recent decades, artists have posed with boards, sung about them, and featured them in performances. Why? Because they know it gives an edge, an aura of "spiritual power." But Scripture says plainly: *"There shall not be found among you… a consulter with familiar spirits, or a wizard, or a necromancer"* (Deuteronomy 18:10–11). The Ouija board isn't a toy—it's a portal.

Occult Symbols in Music

Look closer at concerts, stages, and album covers. The "all-seeing eye" of Horus, pentagrams, inverted crosses—they're everywhere. These symbols come from Egypt, Babylon, and satanic ritual. When millions chant along to songs under flashing occult symbols, it isn't harmless. It's worship.

- The all-seeing eye: linked to Horus in Egypt and later to Freemasonry.

- The pentagram: ancient symbol of invoking spirits.

- The inverted cross: mockery of Christ's crucifixion.

Artists know exactly what they're doing. They're packaging old pagan rituals for mass consumption.

Callout: A halftime show may look like entertainment—but if you swapped the stage for a temple, the rituals would look exactly the same.

Selling the Soul

From Robert Johnson at the crossroads to modern rappers bragging about "selling my soul," the theme hasn't changed. Fame, power, and influence are exchanged for allegiance. The enemy isn't hiding anymore—he's boasting through artists, while the world claps along.

And what happens? Millions sing the words, declare the chants, and repeat the incantations—without realizing they're agreeing with the very spirits behind the music. Words have power, and the devil is using lyrics to bind.

Walk behind the red carpet and you'll find something the cameras never show. Hollywood and the music industry don't just run on talent and money — they run on networks, power structures, and secret societies. For decades, researchers, journalists, and even insiders have noted the influence of fraternal orders, occult sects, and closed-door clubs on who rises and who falls. Whether it's elite parties in hidden mansions, "invite-only" retreats, or industry "initiations," the message is the same: success at the highest levels comes at a price.

These groups aren't new. From the ancient mystery schools of Egypt and Greece to the secret lodges of Europe, elites have always cloaked their rituals in secrecy. When these orders intersect with entertainment, the rituals often masquerade as "branding" or "creative expression." But insiders tell stories of oath-taking, symbolic acts, and moral compromises demanded before an artist gets the full machine behind them. You don't sign just a contract; you enter a fraternity.

Even artists have hinted at it in interviews. Some speak of "selling my soul" or "making a deal." Others describe strange ceremonies at label parties, or being pressured to perform acts that mock faith. While the mainstream press laughs it off, the imagery on stage and in videos tells another story: inverted crosses, Masonic symbols, Egyptian all-seeing eyes, black-and-white checkerboards straight out of lodge floors. They're not accidents. They're signatures.

From a biblical perspective, this isn't surprising. *"The whole world lieth in wickedness"* (1 John 5:19). Secret alliances, oath-bound societies, and occult practices have always been the devil's way of building power structures. When an industry that shapes global culture also traffics in secrecy and ritual, believers should not be naïve. The price of fame may be more than money — it may be spiritual compromise. That's why Paul warned, *"Have no fellowship with the unfruitful works of darkness, but rather reprove them"* (Ephesians 5:11).

Common Symbols and Rituals in Entertainment

1. The All-Seeing Eye

- **Origin:** Ancient Egypt, symbol of Horus, later absorbed into Freemasonry.

- **Modern Use:** Posed over one eye in photos, flashed in music videos, or placed in stage design.

- **Meaning:** Represents hidden knowledge, control, and "illumination."

Callout: When your favorite artist covers one eye, it's not random—it's allegiance to the Eye of Horus, not the God of Scripture.

2. The Checkerboard Floor

- **Origin:** Masonic lodges use black-and-white tiles to symbolize the duality of good and evil.

- **Modern Use:** Music videos, stage sets, and fashion shoots regularly place stars on checkerboard backgrounds.

- **Meaning:** Represents the "balance" of light and darkness—an occult distortion of God's holiness.

3. Inverted Crosses and Pentagrams

- **Origin:** Pagan and satanic rituals mocking the cross and invoking spirits.

- **Modern Use:** Album covers, jewelry, tattoos, or on-stage props.

- **Meaning:** Direct rebellion against Christ and glorification of darkness.

4. Initiation Rituals

- **Origin:** Ancient mystery religions required pledges, sacrifices, and symbolic acts to prove loyalty.

- **Modern Use:** Industry "initiation" may include humiliating acts, public oaths, or performances that blaspheme faith. Some artists admit to "rituals" before signing major contracts.

- **Meaning:** Allegiance to the system—not just to a label, but to a power structure behind it.

5. Mockery of Baptism or Sacrifice

- **Origin:** Pagan rituals often included blood sacrifices or symbolic death-and-rebirth ceremonies.

- **Modern Use:** Artists staging performances where they're "reborn," bathed in fire, or drenched in mock blood. Others act out crucifixions or demonic possession on stage.

- **Meaning:** Substituting God's covenant symbols with counterfeit rituals of allegiance.

6. The Goat and Horned Figures

- **Origin:** Worship of Pan, Baal, and Baphomet in ancient fertility and occult rites.

- **Modern Use:** Flashing horn hand signs, goat-head masks, or explicit references in lyrics.

- **Meaning:** Embracing satanic imagery as a badge of rebellion and power.

Why It Matters

Here's the truth: music is a battleground. What you sing, you confess. What you repeat, you agree with. The enemy uses beats and lyrics to slip in what he could never preach from a pulpit. Paul warned in Ephesians 5:19 to sing "psalms and hymns and spiritual songs," filling ourselves with the Spirit. The world says the opposite: fill yourself with spells, lust, rebellion, and death.

Music isn't neutral. It's either lifting you toward God or dragging you into darkness. And when Christians treat occult imagery, tarot cards, and Ouija boards as "art," we open the door for deception. Behind the smoke machines and auto-tune is the same old lie: *"Bow down and worship me"* (Matthew 4:9).

Call to Action

Entertainment is never neutral. Symbols, rituals, and performances have spiritual weight. When you consume media, ask yourself: Does this lift my eyes to Christ, or does it drag my soul toward darkness? The choice is yours. As Joshua declared: *"Choose you this day whom ye will serve"* (Joshua 24:15).

Questions for Reflection

1. When you see an artist flash a hand sign or pose with one eye covered, do you dismiss it as coincidence, or consider what it might really mean?

2. How do these symbols condition fans—especially children—to accept rebellion against God as normal or entertaining?

3. Why does the Bible repeatedly warn against participating in the "works of darkness" (Ephesians 5:11)?

4. What steps can you take to guard your mind and heart from occult imagery in media?

5. How can believers engage with culture without being shaped by it?

Part 3: Sports and Idolatry

Imagine explaining modern sports to someone from the ancient world. You'd say: "Millions of people paint their faces, scream at the top of their lungs, and cry when strangers in matching jerseys lose a game." The ancient Roman would nod and say, "Ah yes, the Colosseum." Because that's exactly what it is—entertainment elevated to religion.

Think about it. Stadiums are temples. Fans are worshipers. Chants are liturgies. Athletes are gods of flesh and blood, idolized for their strength, speed, and skill. The average believer won't memorize three Scriptures, but they'll recite player stats for the last ten seasons without blinking. If that's not worship, what is?

And it's not just loyalty—it's ritual. From mascots that trace back to pagan animals, to chants that sound eerily like war cries, to millions bowing their heads not to pray but to watch a coin toss—sports culture is drenched in idolatry. The game isn't just a game anymore. It's a religion disguised as recreation.

Stadium Rituals

Sports stadiums are modern temples. Think about it: massive arenas filled with tens of thousands, all chanting in unison, waving banners, and singing anthems. The parallels to ancient cult worship are too obvious to miss. The Romans had gladiator games. The Greeks had the Olympics dedicated to Zeus. Today, we have the Super Bowl.

*Did You Know? The word "fan" is short for "fanatic." That's not just enthusiasm—it's devotion.

Mascots and Pagan Roots

Many team mascots trace back to pagan mythology or animal spirits. The eagle, lion, bear, bull—once sacred symbols of power—now dance across fields and arenas. Ancient cultures believed these animals carried divine strength. Modern culture laughs and calls it "mascots." But the symbolism remains.

Chants and War Cries

The synchronized chants of fans—"DEFENSE! DEFENSE!"—echo ancient battle cries. Whole crowds move in unison, clapping, stomping, shouting. The energy is electric, even spiritual. Instead of invoking God, the ritual channels collective devotion into the game.

Idolatry of Athletes

Imagine a father was sitting in the living room with his son, both dressed head to toe in their team's colors. The boy's room was plastered with posters of his favorite athlete. Jerseys, sneakers, even wristbands—if the player wore it, the boy begged for it. One night, as the game played on, the father noticed his son bowing his head in front of the TV, whispering: *"Please let him win, please let him win."* It wasn't a prayer to God. It was a plea to the universe on behalf of a man who could dunk a ball.

The father chuckled, thinking it was cute. He never stopped to ask why his son could cry when the athlete lost, but never cry over sin. Why his son could memorize every stat, but stumble through a single Bible verse. Without realizing it, the father had discipled his child to worship at the altar of the stadium. The athlete became the boy's hero, priest, and god all at once. And the father, by silence, gave permission.

The father didn't notice that every time the athlete scored, the boy jumped up with hands raised higher than he ever lifted them in church. He didn't realize his son would skip Bible study but never miss a tip-off. When the boy finally said, *"Dad, I want to be just like him,"* the father felt proud, not knowing his son had chosen an idol over the image of Christ.

It mirrors Israel's mistake. The people wanted a king "like the nations" (1 Samuel 8:5), someone to look up to instead of trusting God. The boy wanted a champion in sneakers, not a Savior with scars. Slowly, the family altar had been replaced by a flat-screen altar, and the prayers went not to heaven but to the highlight reel.

Jesus said, *"Where your treasure is, there will your heart be also"* (Matthew 6:21). The boy's treasure was in sneakers, jerseys, and statistics—not in the Word of God. And the father, thinking it was harmless, let the worship grow. By the time he realized the athlete had more influence than Christ, the boy's heart already belonged to the stadium.

The warning is clear: idolatry doesn't always look like a golden calf. Sometimes it looks like a framed jersey on the bedroom wall. Parents must guard their children, because what you laugh off as "just a phase" may be the very thing shaping their soul.

The Greeks worshiped Hercules. The Romans adored gladiators. Today, athletes fill that role. Jerseys with their names, posters on walls, kids imitating their every move. Entire lives revolve around men and women who throw, kick, or dribble a ball. And when athletes fall, it shakes fans like a priest caught in scandal. That's because the athlete wasn't just admired—he was worshiped.

Why It Matters

Sports aren't evil in themselves. Paul even used athletic metaphors to illustrate spiritual truths (1 Corinthians 9:24). But when recreation becomes religion, when cheering becomes worship, when athletes become idols—the line has been crossed.

The Bible warns: *"Little children, keep yourselves from idols"* (1 John 5:21). Yet the church often excuses sports idolatry while condemning every other kind. The question isn't whether you watch the game. The question is: who gets your worship—God, or the gods of the stadium?

Call to Action

Sports themselves are not sin. But when athletes replace Christ as our heroes, when stadiums steal our devotion, when chants drown out our prayers—that's idolatry. Scripture calls us to run the race that matters: *"Looking unto Jesus, the author and finisher of our faith"* (Hebrews 12:2). The choice isn't between winning and losing a game. It's between serving the gods of the stadium or the living God.

Questions for Reflection

1. Have sports in your life ever crossed from recreation into idolatry? How can you tell the difference?

2. What kind of passion and devotion do you give to teams and athletes compared to your devotion to Christ?

3. How might children learn who (or what) to worship by watching the way adults treat sports?

4. If stadiums are modern temples, what does it say about our culture's priorities?

5. How can you enjoy sports in balance without letting them steal your time, worship, or witness?

Part 4: Fraternities and Sororities

A college freshman walked nervously into a dimly lit room. Candles flickered, blindfolds were passed out, and upperclassmen in robes whispered instructions. He thought he had signed up for friendship, parties, and networking. Instead, he found himself kneeling before a crest, chanting oaths he didn't understand. Someone poured water over his head, someone else made him recite lines, and then they all cheered: "Welcome, brother!" The next day, he laughed it off, calling it tradition.

But as the weeks went on, he noticed the rituals never stopped. Secret handshakes, chants in Greek, oaths to protect the fraternity above all else. His friends wore letters like holy garments and shouted chants as if invoking unseen powers. He realized the fraternity wasn't just a club—it was a religion.

Years later, he looked back and asked himself: Why did I agree to bow, pledge, and chant without thinking? The answer was simple: the rituals felt fun, powerful, even sacred. That's how paganism works. It doesn't show up with horns and fire—it shows up in robes, oaths, and Greek letters at a campus initiation.

Modern fraternities and sororities trace their lineage to **ancient mystery religions and secret societies**. The Greek letters aren't random—they connect back to the Greek pantheon, where each god represented wisdom, war, or pleasure. Initiation ceremonies, blindfolds, chants, and oaths all echo rites of passage from pagan cults.

Many members of fraternities and sororities proudly claim the name of Christ. They sing hymns, pray in public, and call themselves believers. Yet, when initiation night comes, they bow blindfolded, chant Greek oaths, and pledge lifelong loyalty to an organization above all else. The contradiction is undeniable. Jesus warned directly against such practices: *"Swear not at all... But let your communication be, Yea, yea; Nay, nay"* (Matthew 5:34–37). Yet, fraternity and sorority members swear elaborate oaths of secrecy and loyalty, binding themselves to human institutions with promises God never sanctioned.

These rituals also thrive on **darkness and secrecy**—symbols of "hidden wisdom" borrowed from the mystery religions of Greece and Rome. But the Word of God says, *"For every one that doeth evil hateth the light, neither cometh to the light, lest his deeds should be reproved"* (John 3:20). Paul takes it further: *"Have no fellowship with the unfruitful works of darkness, but rather reprove them"* (Ephesians 5:11). Yet, initiation rites are carried out in dimly lit rooms, with blindfolds, secrecy, and symbolism that directly contradicts the call to walk in the light of Christ.

Greek organizations often speak of "rebirth" into the fraternity or sorority—through rituals that mimic death and resurrection. Yet the Bible says true rebirth comes only through Christ: *"Except a man be born again, he cannot see the kingdom of God"* (John 3:3). Any imitation is counterfeit. In the same way, loyalty to "brothers" or "sisters" in the organization often supersedes loyalty to Christ's body, the church. But Scripture warns: *"Ye cannot serve God and mammon"* (Matthew 6:24). To swear allegiance to any other fellowship above Christ is to split your loyalty between two masters.

The tragedy is that many believers convince themselves it's harmless. They argue, "It's just tradition. It doesn't mean anything." But God's people said the same thing when they bowed to Baal and Asherah—"This is just culture." Yet God called it idolatry. *"Thou shalt have no other gods before me"* (Exodus 20:3). When Christians participate in oaths, rituals, and covenants rooted in pagan traditions, they step into the same pattern Israel fell into again and again. The truth is hard but clear: professing Christ while pledging to idols cannot stand. *"Ye cannot drink the cup of the Lord, and the cup of devils"* (1 Corinthians 10:21).

- **Oaths:** Members pledge lifelong loyalty, echoing ancient vows to gods and idols. Jesus warned, *"Swear not at all... but let your 'Yes' be 'Yes' and your 'No,' 'No'"* (Matthew 5:34–37).

- **Blindfolds and darkness:** Used in secret initiations to symbolize "ignorance to enlightenment," just as mystery religions promised hidden wisdom.

- **Greek letters and names:** Many directly invoke pagan deities or ideals tied to Greek philosophy.

- **Chants and rituals:** Modeled after incantations, designed to bind members together spiritually.

*Did You Know? The very word *sorority* means "sisterhood" but often borrows imagery from goddess cults of fertility and harvest.

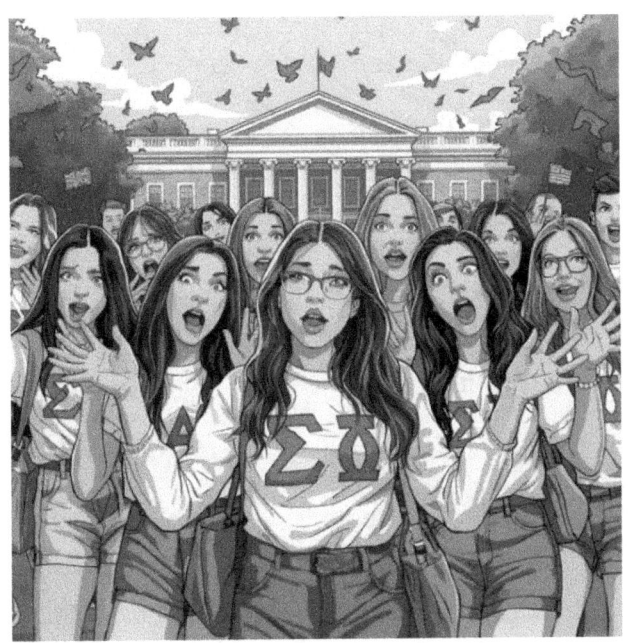

Why It Matters

Most students join for social life or networking, not realizing they're pledging allegiance through **ritual acts rooted in paganism**. What looks like harmless tradition is often a spiritual covenant. The Bible warns: *"Be not unequally yoked together with unbelievers… what agreement hath the temple of God with idols?"* (2 Corinthians 6:14–16).

The truth is, modern fraternities and sororities are not just clubs. They're cults of loyalty, designed to mimic ancient initiations. And when believers take those oaths, they bind themselves to something God never ordained.

Observations & Context

1. **Use of Greek Letters & Secrecy:**

    o Many fraternities and sororities adopted **Greek letters** to suggest classical learning, philosophy, mystery, or wisdom.

    o Their rituals and structure often draw from older secret society traditions (like Freemasonry) and mystery cults.

2. **Exclusion & Formation of Black Greek Life:**

    o Black students were barred or heavily discriminated against from the older Greek organizations, so they founded the NPHC / "Divine Nine" to create their own space for excellence, fellowship, and activism.

    o These organizations became important platforms for leadership, civil rights, community service, and cultural identity.

3. **Secret Rituals & Oaths:**

    o Many Greek organizations have secret rituals, oaths, initiation ceremonies, hand signs, etc., aspects that echo mystery religions or clandestine societies.

- o Because of the secrecy, many of their traditions and ceremonies are not public or widely documented.

4. **Cultural Influence & Legacy:**

   - o These organizations have influence well beyond campus: alumni networks, politics, business, social leadership, philanthropy, media, etc.

   - o Black Greek-letter organizations in particular have had a major role in the civil rights movement and African American leadership.

Brief History on Some of the Major Fraternities and Sororities

1. Phi Beta Kappa (1776, College of William & Mary)

- **Origins:** The very first U.S. Greek-letter society. Founded during the Revolutionary era, its structure borrowed directly from European secret societies, especially Freemasonry.

- **Rituals & Symbols:** Secret handshakes, mottos in Greek, closed meetings, and coded badges. Its three letters stand for a Greek motto meaning *"Love of learning is the guide of life."*

- **Pagan Parallels:** The use of secrecy, Greek philosophy, and initiation oaths mirrors the **mystery schools of Greece**. What began as a literary society became a **quasi-religious order** of intellectual elitism.

2. Alpha Phi Alpha (1906, Cornell University)

- **Origins:** First Black Greek-letter fraternity, founded when Black students were excluded from mainstream Greek life.

- **Rituals & Symbols:** Its imagery often incorporates Egyptian motifs (the sphinx, pyramids). Members pledge loyalty through initiation ceremonies and secret oaths.

- **Pagan Parallels:** Egyptology was tied to ancient pagan worship (sun gods, afterlife rituals). While intended to affirm Black heritage, the **Sphinx and pyramid** are direct echoes of pharaonic religion, which Scripture identifies with idolatry (Exodus 12:12).

3. Alpha Kappa Alpha (1908, Howard University)

- **Origins:** First Black Greek-letter sorority, emphasizing "service to all mankind."

- **Rituals & Symbols:** Uses ivy leaf symbolism, secret ceremonies, and oaths to the organization.

- **Pagan Parallels:** Ivy was sacred to **Dionysus**, the Greek god of wine and ecstasy, symbolizing loyalty and eternal life apart from Christ. Wearing ivy crowns was part of Dionysian festivals.

4. Kappa Alpha Psi & Omega Psi Phi (1911)

- **Origins:** Both fraternities arose during segregation, creating networks for Black men.

- **Rituals & Symbols:** Both use strong ritualistic initiation ceremonies, Greek names, and step shows that mimic military and cultic drills.

- **Pagan Parallels:** Oaths of lifelong loyalty echo the **binding vows of ancient cult initiates**. Chants and step rituals often resemble call-and-response worship in mystery religions.

5. Delta Sigma Theta (1913, Howard University)

- **Origins:** Sorority founded by women who broke away from Alpha Kappa Alpha. Known for social justice work and community organizing.

- **Rituals & Symbols:** Uses the pyramid as a central emblem. Members participate in secret ceremonies and public rituals like the "Elephant Walk."

- **Pagan Parallels:** The pyramid is an Egyptian religious symbol tied to sun worship and afterlife. The **triangle** itself was used in Greek and Roman mysticism to represent divine power.

6. Predominantly White "Social" Fraternities (e.g., Sigma Chi, Delta Upsilon, Phi Delta Theta)

- **Origins:** Sprang up in the 1800s from college literary and debating societies, but deliberately added secrecy, initiation rites, and ritualized brotherhood modeled after Freemasonry.

- **Rituals & Symbols:** Blindfold initiations, oaths of secrecy, symbolic "death and rebirth" ceremonies, and ritual books with prayers not addressed to God but to the fraternity.

- **Pagan Parallels:** These practices are nearly identical to **Greek mystery cult initiations** (Eleusinian Mysteries, Dionysian rites), where initiates were blindfolded, taken through secret trials, and reborn into the group.

Call to Action

Brothers and sisters, let me speak plainly: Christ does not share His throne. You cannot kneel before an altar of Greek letters on Friday night and then kneel before Christ as if nothing happened. Jesus said, *"No man can serve two masters"* (Matthew 6:24). When you pledge yourself to a fraternity or sorority, swearing lifelong loyalty through oaths and rituals, you are binding yourself to a covenant that Scripture never allows. The Word of God declares, *"Swear not at all"* (Matthew 5:34). Yet these organizations demand oaths of secrecy and allegiance. Who will you believe—the Word of Christ, or the word of culture?

Fraternities and sororities promise community, loyalty, and identity—but only Christ provides those in truth. The church is already a brotherhood and sisterhood sealed by the blood of Jesus, not by oaths to idols. Scripture calls us to renounce the hidden works of darkness and walk in the light. If you are a believer in Christ, you must ask: **Am I pledging my soul to culture, or to the Kingdom?**

Questions for Reflection

1. If Jesus warned against swearing oaths, what does it mean when Christians swear lifelong pledges to fraternities and sororities?

2. Why do you think these organizations keep their rituals in darkness and secrecy?

3. How does joining a Greek-letter group affect a believer's loyalty to the church, which is the true body of Christ?

4. What does it say about our priorities if we're more devoted to "brothers" and "sisters" in a fraternity or sorority than to fellow disciples of Christ?

5. How can a believer honor heritage and community without taking part in rituals rooted in paganism?

Chapter 5
Part V: Breaking the Strongholds

There was once a man who set up a little shrine in his living room. He placed a statue of a bull on the table, lit candles, and bowed down before it. His neighbor walked in and asked, "Why are you talking to a cow?" The man, completely serious, said, "This cow controls the rain, my money, and maybe even my love life." The neighbor shook his head and replied, "Friend, that cow doesn't even moo. You bought it at the flea market."

The next week, another neighbor came by and found him kneeling before a carved piece of wood. "What's this one?" she asked. He smiled proudly: "This log protects my family." The neighbor tapped the idol, and the thing tipped over like a domino. "So your god just got knocked out by my pinky finger," she said. He quickly set it upright and whispered, "Shhh, don't make him angry."

Meanwhile, his kids in the other room were laughing hysterically. "Dad, you're bowing to a bull and a block of wood when we've got Wi-Fi that answers faster than your idols. And didn't you preach last week that the living God split the Red Sea?" The man paused, scratching his head. Suddenly the truth hit him: worshipping false gods wasn't just wrong—it was ridiculous. The only thing his idols controlled was how much dust gathered on the shelf.

And that's exactly what the prophets said long ago. Isaiah mocked the idol-maker who chops down a tree, burns half of it for firewood, and then bows to the other half as his "god" (Isaiah 44:13–20). Psalm 115 says it plain: *"Their idols are silver and gold, the work of men's hands. They have mouths, but they speak not: eyes have they, but they see not... they that make them are like unto them; so is every one that trusteth in them."* In other words, idols are powerless—and the people who trust them become just as blind and mute.

So the next time someone bows to a statue, a logo, or even a celebrity on a stage, remember: they're talking to a cow that can't moo and a log that tips over. Meanwhile, the living God speaks, hears, saves, and reigns forever. False gods may be funny, but following them is no joke.

What the Bible Says About False Gods

From Genesis to Revelation, the Bible is crystal clear: God does not tolerate rivals. *"Thou shalt have no other gods before me"* (Exodus 20:3). Israel was warned again and again not to call on the names of foreign gods (Exodus 23:13), not to learn the ways of the nations (Jeremiah 10:2), and not to mix the holy with the profane (Ezekiel 22:26). Paul repeats it: *"The things which the Gentiles sacrifice, they sacrifice to devils, and not to God"* (1 Corinthians 10:20). Behind every idol is not just a myth, but a spirit.

Calling on false gods isn't harmless tradition—it is spiritual adultery. God told Israel, *"Make no mention of the name of other gods, neither let it be heard out of thy mouth"* (Joshua 23:7). He will not share His glory with Baal, Zeus, or Santa Claus. Yeshua Himself warned that no one can serve two masters (Matthew 6:24). To invoke the names, symbols, or rituals of idols is to step into covenant with them. Scripture calls this what it is: idolatry.

From Pagan Customs to God's Commandments

But God didn't just say what *not* to do—He gave His people holy days, rhythms of life, and a calendar rooted in His truth. The Sabbath, the Feasts of the LORD, and His appointed times were designed to keep His people aligned with His covenant. "And God said, Let there be lights in the firmament of the heaven to divide the day from the night; and let them be for signs, and for seasons, and for days, and years" Genesis 1:14.

God gave us a calendar with the moon cycle representing our months.

Leviticus 23-

- **The Sabbath** reminds us God is Creator and Redeemer. It's a day of rest in Him (Exodus 20:8–11; Deuteronomy 5:15).

- **Passover** points directly to Jesus as the Lamb who takes away sin (1 Corinthians 5:7).

- **Unleavened Bread** teaches holiness—removing sin as we follow Christ.

- **Firstfruits** is fulfilled in Jesus' resurrection (1 Corinthians 15:20).

- **Pentecost (Shavuot)** points to the outpouring of the Holy Spirit (Acts 2).

- **Trumpets, Atonement, Tabernacles** all point ahead to Christ's return, judgment, and eternal dwelling with His people (Zechariah 14; Revelation 21).

While the world clings to man-made traditions—Christmas trees, Easter bunnies, birthday candles—God has given His people holy days that point directly to His Son. Replacing the traditions of men with the commandments of God is not a burden. It's freedom.

Pulling Down Strongholds

Paul wrote, *"For the weapons of our warfare are not carnal, but mighty through God to the pulling down of strongholds"* (2 Corinthians 10:4). What are these strongholds? They are false beliefs, pagan customs, and cultural idols that exalt themselves against the knowledge of God. They are the rituals we excuse as harmless but which slowly shape our loyalty.

To pull them down, we must first **recognize their roots**. When we see a holiday, ritual, or tradition, we ask: Does this come from the Word of God, or from the world of idols? Second, we must **renounce what is false**. That means turning from oaths, symbols, and celebrations that compete with Christ. Finally, we must **reclaim identity in truth**—not in secret societies, sports idols, or cultural fables, but in the Word and Spirit of God.

Breaking strongholds isn't about losing fun. It's about gaining freedom. It's about walking in the covenant God designed, rooted in His holy calendar, anchored in His Son, and filled with His Spirit. When believers reclaim this, the body of Christ is strengthened, and the true commonwealth of Israel—every disciple in Messiah—rises in unity and power.

Many people grow up believing traditions are sacred simply because they are old. Families celebrate every holiday the culture prescribes. Trees go up, cakes are baked, candles are blown out, colors are worn, and chants are repeated—without anyone stopping to ask, *"Where did this come from?"* or *"Does God approve of this?"* The answer is usually, "This is just what we do. It's tradition." And for countless households, that's enough to keep them bound.

Even after some begin reading the Bible, the pull of tradition remains powerful. When Scriptures against idolatry and pagan customs appear, the natural instinct is to explain them away—because admitting the truth would mean confessing that entire ways of life have been shaped by something other than God. That's how strong tradition is. It doesn't just dictate actions; it shapes identity. And the moment anyone questions it, they feel as if they are betraying family, culture, or even themselves.

But Jesus said, *"If any man come to me, and hate not his father, and mother, and wife, and children, and brethren, and sisters, yea, and his own life also, he cannot be my disciple"* (Luke 14:26). He was not commanding literal hatred of family—He was demanding ultimate loyalty. In other words, if family traditions conflict with God's Word, disciples must choose Him above even father or mother. That is the dividing line between culture and covenant.

Tradition, for many, becomes a stronghold—defended not by truth, but by fear of letting go. But when people surrender those traditions, they discover real freedom. That's when Paul's words come alive: *"The weapons of our warfare are not carnal, but mighty through God to the pulling down of strong holds"* (2 Corinthians 10:4). Breaking tradition is never easy; it can feel like losing part of one's identity. But in reality, it's tearing down chains. Our real identity was never meant to be in cultural customs—it was always meant to be in Christ.

Final Word

The gods of this world will always demand oaths, rituals, and worship. But Jesus Christ already paid the price, already sealed the covenant, already tore the veil. The call is simple: renounce the false, embrace the true, and walk in the freedom of the King. *"Choose you this day whom ye will serve… but as for me and my house, we will serve the LORD"* (Joshua 24:15).

About the Author

Karajah Yashar is a writer, counselor, and publisher with a passion for uncovering truths often hidden in plain sight. He earned his degree in Anthropology, a field that sharpened his eye for culture, history, and the ways belief systems shape human behavior. Karajah has worked in respected institutions such as Rutgers University, the University of Central Florida, and The Transition House, where he served as a counselor for incarcerated men, helping them confront personal strongholds and rebuild their lives.

In 2016, Karajah founded **Passed Over Press** (formerly Blackstone Publishing), a publishing company devoted to producing books, videos, and workshops that highlight knowledge often "passed over" in mainstream religious and cultural circles. His mission is to restore forgotten truths, challenge long-standing traditions, and provide resources that strengthen faith and identity in Christ.

Karajah Yashar continues to write, teach, and publish works that bring clarity to complex topics, combining scholarly insight with a passion for truth. His voice calls readers to examine tradition, embrace Scripture, and walk boldly in the covenant of the Most High.